THE YALE DRAMA SERIES

David Charles Horn Foundation

The Yale Drama Series is funded by the generous support of the David Charles Horn Foundation, established in 2003 by Francine Horn to honor the memory of her husband, David. In keeping with David Horn's lifetime commitment to the written word, the David Charles Horn Foundation commemorates his aspirations and achievements by supporting new initiatives in the literary and dramatic arts.

Grenadine

NEIL WECHSLER

Foreword by Edward Albee

YALE UNIVERSITY PRESS   NEW HAVEN & LONDON

Copyright © 2009 by Neil Wechsler.
Foreword copyright © 2009 by Edward Albee.

Set in ITC Galliard type by Duke & Company, Devon, Pennsylvania.
Printed in the United States of America by Sheridan Books, Ann Arbor,
Michigan.

Library of Congress Cataloging-in-Publication Data
Wechsler, Neil, 1974–
Grenadine / Neil Wechsler ; foreword by Edward Albee.
p.   cm. — (Yale drama series)
ISBN 978-0-300-14992-0 (alk. paper)
1. Male friendship—Drama. 2. Voyages and travels—Drama. I. Title.
PS3623.E3977G74 2009
812'.6—dc22   2009009673

A catalogue record for this book is available from the British Library.

This paper meets the requirements of ANSI/NISO Z39.48-1992
(Permanence of Paper).

10 9 8 7 6 5 4 3 2 1

Contents

Foreword: Judgment Day 2, *by Edward Albee* vi

Grenadine 1

Foreword
Judgment Day 2

A s I wrote last year in my report on the inaugural contest, I am not certain that the play which I have chosen to win the Yale Drama Series, and the accompanying David C. Horn Prize, co-sponsored by Yale University Press and Yale Repertory Theatre, is necessarily the best play of the four hundred and forty-five submitted.

How can this be? Well, I did not read all of the plays. There are two reasons for this—my sanity and my time. My sanity first: I have judged enough play contests and read enough new plays generally to know that maybe one in twenty of the plays submitted to any contest is worth the reading, and that we playwrights are in sufficient despair over the condition of theatre without having our tenuous grasp on life-force diminished by the pummelings of the mediocre and the truly hopeless.

Then my time: see "my sanity" above.

What to do? What I *did* was, have chosen six young theatre professionals—playwrights, mostly—whose work and minds I could respect and whose objectivity I could trust to winnow the pile down to a relative "precious few"—thirty-five or so—and read *them*—thoroughly and carefully.

This is not an ideal solution, but what is one to do? There is no perfect way around four hundred and forty-five scripts and one final judge, but I feel we have solved it as wisely—if imperfectly—as could be done, and if there are finer plays than our winner in the four hundred and ten plays I *didn't* read, my congratulations to their authors. They are undoubtedly extraordinary writers, and their time will come.

Now to the chase.

What standards did I employ in judging the plays I read? Well, the predictable, of course:

Have I read this play before? (Interesting how often the borrowings tend to be from minor plays.)

Can I read to the end of it without losing consciousness? (How often I would refresh myself—coffee, perhaps; stand up, walk around.)

Am I learning anything from this play? (Anything provocative and illuminating, that is?)

Are the questions the play poses sufficiently interesting to warrant the paucity of answers provided? (Often—perhaps oddly—the questions are almost always more interesting than the answers provided. In theory, at least, a play of only questions can be profoundly involving.)

Does this play stretch my mind, open vistas of yet unexplored dramatic concepts? (Well, *that* doesn't happen very often, *does* it?! And when it does we are grateful beyond thanks.)

Is this play just so "good" at what it does that we are tricked (almost!) into thinking it matters?

Is this absolutely chaotic and anti-dramatic mess of a play really as exciting as it seems?

And so on.

Ideally a play should be so fresh in its ideas and execution that we are breathless, for it is clearly the first play we have ever read! Or is it merely honorable, intellectually and emotionally engaging, structurally persuasive on its own terms, and worthy of a mumbled "Well, now, *that* wasn't bad!" This last describes most of the "good" plays one reads. The exceptional is truly rare—one out of a hundred, maybe? One out of two hundred?

The plays submitted to me in each of the past two years ran the gamut, of course. Some were tiresome retreads; some indicated no intuitive understanding of dramatic structure; some were really essays in borrowed clothing; a few were laughable in their efforts to be shocking; some others were intelligent and sincere but hampered by their belief that play-writing ended with mid-period Ibsen; a few were all emotion and nothing else; a few were hobbled by crippling Mamet-isms, some by (intended?) stylelessness; and some were . . . O.K., if hardly exceptional.

This year there was one that really took my attention and held it: *Grenadine*, by Neil Wechsler.

I found it highly original; it kept me fully awake; I learned quite a bit; both the questions the play asks and the answers it proposes are provocative; the play stretched my mind.

If I have one reservation it is that my favorite character, Pyx, vanishes (through apparent drowning) in scene 6 and reappears only quite near the end of the play, diminished in wonderfulness (perhaps drowning, apparent or otherwise, does this) but able to recover in time to say the play's lovely last line.

I look forward to seeing this play in production—a good production worthy of its creator's imagination. After all, only mediocrity deserves mediocrity, and our theatre is far too occupied with perpetuating mediocrity as it is.

Edward Albee
New York City
August 2008

Grenadine

Cast of Characters

(in order of appearance)

PRISMATIC

GROVE

SCONCE

PYX

OLD WOMAN ON A BENCH (Actress 1)

OLD WOMAN SELLING BERRIES (Actress 1)

OLD MAN SELLING WATERMELONS (Actor 1)

MASTER OF CEREMONIES (Actor 2)

ELDER DUCK (Actress 1)

YOUNGER DUCK (Actress 2)

TURTLE (Actor 1)

NESSA DOTSUN (Actress 2)

FERGUS DOTSUN (Actor 2)

OLD MAN SITTING ON THE SIDE OF THE ROAD (Actor 1)

OLD WOMAN SELLING TOMATOES (Actress 1)

OLD MAN SELLING TOMATOES (Actor 1)

GIRL (Actress 2)

BOY (Actor 2)

MOTHER (Actress 1)

FATHER (Actor 1)

SISTER OF THE BRIDE (Actress 2)

FATHER OF THE BRIDE (Actor 1)

MOTHER OF THE BRIDE (Actress 1)

OLD WOMAN PAINTING A LANDSCAPE (Actress 1)

BEEKEEPER (Actor 2)

TWO-LEGGED DACHSHUND (Actor 1)

COOK (Actor 2)

FISHERMAN (Actor 2)

GENTLEMAN (Actor 2)

YOUNG MOTHER (Actress 2)

A Note About the Staging: The main characters enter and exit many times throughout the play, and the transitions must be handled creatively to maintain the continuity of their journey. The passage of time should be represented by a change of lighting: sun breaking through fog, sunny skies becoming overcast, late afternoon becoming sunset. The colors should be intrinsic to the mood of the play and help create the abstract, pastoral world the play seeks to establish. The secondary characters ease the transitions by setting the stage with their props while the main characters are offstage. Much of the action is mimed by the actors, and some takes place offstage, as indicated in the stage directions. The staging should always seek to illuminate the main characters' bumbling perseverance.

Scene One

PRISMATIC, GROVE, SCONCE, and PYX *stand at a bus stop beside the* OLD WOMAN ON A BENCH. PRISMATIC *wears red,* GROVE *green,* SCONCE *yellow, and* PYX *blue. They each wear an item of the other three colors.* GROVE *holds a fiddle.*

PRISMATIC   I will soon be with you, Grenadine!

GROVE   We are going back for her?

PRISMATIC   Round as the sun, and I love her!

GROVE   We have been on a prison farm three years because of her.

PRISMATIC   Round, round, everywhere round!

GROVE   The engagement ring we stole.

PRISMATIC   My gossamer gay gosling with your gems aglow!

GROVE   Which she threw back at you.

PRISMATIC   Grenadine! Do you hear my cries and my shouts and my lamentations and my fears?

OLD WOMAN ON A BENCH   I hear them.

SCONCE   Be not afraid, Artemis, we are docile.

OLD WOMAN ON A BENCH Why do you call me
Artemis?

GROVE He has been reading nothing but mythology
and folklore on the prison farm.

SCONCE Artemis, goddess of the hunt and of the chase
and of our freedom.

PYX I am this freedom.

OLD WOMAN ON A BENCH What has he been
reading?

GROVE Religion. He equates himself with all things.

PRISMATIC Grenadine!

OLD WOMAN ON A BENCH What about him?

GROVE Love poetry.

OLD WOMAN ON A BENCH And you?

GROVE Science.

OLD WOMAN ON A BENCH What have you learned?

GROVE The common ancestry of the animals: all of us
evolving from algae, bacteria, sponges, and trilobites over
thousands of years.

OLD WOMAN ON A BENCH Is it not millions of
years?

GROVE It is possible. I have no conception of time and
am bewildered by dates.

OLD WOMAN ON A BENCH   Perhaps it was not three
years you were on the prison farm.

GROVE   (*To* PRISMATIC.) It was not three years?

SCONCE   It was not a prison farm, it was Demeter's
garden, and we were its guardians.

PYX   I am this guardian.

PRISMATIC   When will this bus arrive?

OLD WOMAN ON A BENCH   There is no bus. It
stopped running years ago.

PRISMATIC   Then why are you waiting for it?

OLD WOMAN ON A BENCH   I am waiting for
nothing. I enjoy the scene and the conversations of the
men who congregate here, released from the prison farm,
filled with dreams.

PYX   I am these dreams.

PRISMATIC   Can you point the way to the coast?

OLD WOMAN ON A BENCH   I have never been to
the coast, but this road will take you away from here and
might lead to a road to the coast.

PRISMATIC   I will soon be with you, Grenadine!

PRISMATIC *exits.* SCONCE, PYX, *and* GROVE *follow. The* OLD
WOMAN *remains. The lights fade.*

Scene Two

The OLD WOMAN SELLING BERRIES *is standing at a
fruit stand on the side of the road. She is wearing a shawl.*
PRISMATIC, SCONCE, GROVE, *and* PYX *enter.* PRISMATIC
picks out four baskets of berries and hands the OLD WOMAN
money. The OLD WOMAN *reaches under the table and sets
out some jars of jam.* PRISMATIC *turns to the others.*

PRISMATIC   Do we like jam?

SCONCE   There are few things finer than jam.

PRISMATIC *hands the* OLD WOMAN *more money. She reaches
under the table and sets out some pie.* PRISMATIC *turns to
the others.*

PRISMATIC   Do we like pie?

SCONCE   Pie is one of those things.

PRISMATIC   One of what things?

SCONCE   Finer than jam.

PRISMATIC *hands the* OLD WOMAN *more money. She sweeps
the rest of the berries into the center of the table.* PRISMATIC
turns to the others, who nod. PRISMATIC *hands the* OLD
WOMAN *more money, and picks up the rest of the berries. The*
OLD WOMAN *folds up her table and exits. The men stack
the food in their arms and, trying to keep their stacks steady,
exit. While offstage, the men are heard dropping, squashing,*

and splattering their berries, pies, and jams. They reenter
with nothing.

PRISMATIC   We are not having the best of success
eating, and we are running out of money.

SCONCE   Money is not of consequence.

PRISMATIC   We will not be able to buy anything.

SCONCE   What good have our purchases done us so far?

PRISMATIC   Can we blame the purchases?

SCONCE   I am not blaming them. I am merely not
crediting them.

GROVE   We ate well on the prison farm.

SCONCE   Demeter's garden, you mean.

PRISMATIC   Demeter! Greek goddess of vegetation!

SCONCE   Mother of Persephone, whom Hades abducted
and made queen of the underworld.

GROVE   She did not wish to marry him?

SCONCE   She starved herself beside him until Zeus
decreed that she only had to spend six months a year there;
the rest she could spend in the garden.

PYX   I am this renewal.

GROVE   Explain it to me, then.

PRISMATIC   Play your fiddle.

GROVE *plays his fiddle.*

PYX   I am this music.

The OLD MAN SELLING WATERMELONS *enters, pushing a wheelbarrow.* PRISMATIC *gives him money.* PRISMATIC *and the others each pick out a watermelon. The* OLD MAN *exits.*

PRISMATIC   We have no knife.

SCONCE   Can we not simply throw them against the ground?

PRISMATIC   They will explode in all directions.

SCONCE   Then we will find one.

PRISMATIC   They are heavy.

SCONCE   You must have fortitude.

GROVE   They were easier to eat in Demeter's garden.

PRISMATIC   It was a prison farm!

PYX   I am this ambiguity.

They exit. The lights fade.

Scene Three

An inclined plane spans the stage. PRISMATIC, SCONCE, GROVE, *and* PYX *enter with watermelons, struggling to ascend the hill, breathing heavily.*

PRISMATIC   Do the rest of you perceive this incline, too?

SCONCE   It is the weight.

PRISMATIC   I am certain it is a hill.

SCONCE   Try not to complain.

PYX   I am this hill.

GROVE   Flatten it out, if you would.

PRISMATIC   We have been on a plain for days. Now, with these watermelons, we have a hill.

SCONCE   Without the watermelon, you would still think it a plain, and since the watermelon has nothing to do with the slope, it is still a plain.

PRISMATIC   It looks like a hill to me.

They struggle on, hardly advancing.

PRISMATIC   We will rest here for a minute.

*He sets the watermelon down. The others do the same. The
watermelons start to roll down the hill. The men do not
notice at first, then turn and run after them. The lights fade,
then rise on an empty stage. The men enter, panting, without
the watermelons, and put their hands on their knees.*

PRISMATIC   (*To* SCONCE.) Do you deny it is a hill now?

SCONCE   It is a plain, at a different angle.

PRISMATIC   The different angle is why it is not a plain!

SCONCE   Only from your perspective.

PRISMATIC   I speak from my perspective!

SCONCE   That is your shortcoming.

PRISMATIC   From what perspective do you speak?

SCONCE   The one of objectivity.

PRISMATIC   Demeter's garden!

SCONCE   Goddess of the soil and of the grain and of
the pure.

PRISMATIC   I do not know why I contend.

SCONCE   Nor I.

GROVE   I do not recall a Demeter or a Persephone in
the garden.

SCONCE   Demeter and her daughter always wear
disguises. Persephone was dressed as a maiden when
Hades captured her.

GROVE   I do not recall any maiden.

SCONCE   She had strayed too far from her companions.

PYX   I am this loss.

SCONCE   Her mother looked for her with a pair of torches and set fire to the fields so that there was famine throughout the kingdom.

GROVE   For three years?

PRISMATIC   We shall not mention this matter again until we have eaten.

PYX   I am this silence.

SCONCE   We can fish in the stream.

PRISMATIC   Have you tackle in your trousers?

SCONCE   We will sharpen some sticks.

PRISMATIC   Had we a knife we would be eating the watermelons.

SCONCE   We will use rocks.

PRISMATIC   On the fish?

SCONCE   On the sticks.

PRISMATIC   Have you done this before, then?

SCONCE *picks up sticks, hands them out.*

PRISMATIC   (*Indicating his stick.*) I could not kill an ant with this.

SCONCE   You do not have to.

He picks up rocks, hands them out.

PRISMATIC   How am I to sharpen my stick if the rock itself is not sharp?

SCONCE   How are you to do anything if you keep complaining?

SCONCE, GROVE, *and* PYX *sharpen their sticks with their rocks;* PRISMATIC, *grumbling, sharpens his. They approach the front of the stage.*

PRISMATIC   All we need now is for a fish to jump out of the stream and lie still for us while we poke it to death with our twigs.

SCONCE   You scoff at the truth.

PRISMATIC   (*Raising his stick.*) *This* is the truth?

SCONCE   And you scoff at it. Now be quiet, or you will scare the fish.

PRISMATIC   On the contrary. When the fish see us standing here with these twigs they will swim over to laugh at us.

SCONCE *raises his stick to strike. The others do the same.*

PRISMATIC   I am an idiot!

SCONCE   Silence!

PYX   I am this fish.

GROVE   Stop swimming so quickly.

PRISMATIC *strikes at a fish, and his stick breaks.*

PRISMATIC Grenadine!

SCONCE You were too hasty, and now you have driven him away.

PRISMATIC Grenadine!

SCONCE Shhh!

PRISMATIC (*Indicating the stream.*) Look, he has brought a friend to share in this farce.

SCONCE *surveys the fish. With a vigorous movement he drives his stick into the water.* GROVE *and* PYX *do the same.* SCONCE *puts a foot in the stream and makes another foray. He hurls his stick at the fish. He dives in.* GROVE, PYX, *and* PRISMATIC *plunge in after him, and the four of them attack the fish simultaneously. The lights dim. The men get out of the water and sit on the bank, shivering, as the lights continue to dim and finally fade to darkness.*

PRISMATIC Grenadine!

A wolf howls.

PRISMATIC Here I am!

SCONCE Wolves do not attack humans.

PRISMATIC To hell with you!

GROVE He is right about the wolves.

PRISMATIC To hell with you, too!

PYX I am this hell.

SCONCE   The sun will be up soon.

PRISMATIC   Soon! Soon!

SCONCE   Whereupon our clothes will begin to dry.

PRISMATIC   If we had not gone swimming!

SCONCE   I did not force you.

PRISMATIC   You gave me a twig!

SCONCE   We will talk in the morning.

The lights rise slowly on the four men, shivering.

PRISMATIC   Soon! Soon!

SCONCE   The sun is here, is it not?

PRISMATIC   Our skin is blue, and we have not eaten since the prison farm.

GROVE   I thought we were not to speak of it until we had eaten.

PRISMATIC   We are not speaking of it.

SCONCE   Of Demeter's garden, rather.

PYX   I am these contradictions.

GROVE   We can go into the woods. I can lure a rabbit with my fiddle.

PRISMATIC   Like Pan?

SCONCE   Pan played a reed pipe, not a fiddle.

GROVE   I have studied rabbits. Their flesh is tender, and with the fur we can make mittens for Grenadine.

SCONCE   (*To* PRISMATIC.) I did not know you were giving her mittens.

PRISMATIC   I am not giving her mittens!

GROVE   It is a loving gift and will not lead to the place of which we cannot speak.

PYX   I am this past.

GROVE *exits. The others follow. The lights dim to overcast skies. The men reenter.*

GROVE   Crouch behind those trees. When the rabbit comes, pounce on him.

PRISMATIC   There is no saving us.

SCONCE   We will try it. If it does not work, and you are still hungry, we will look for food elsewhere.

PRISMATIC   How would I not still be hungry if it does not work?

SCONCE   Sometimes hunger passes.

PRISMATIC   It passes when you eat.

SCONCE   Sometimes it just passes.

GROVE   Continue your discussion later. For now, crouch behind those trees.

PRISMATIC, SCONCE, *and* PYX *crouch.* GROVE *plays. A few seconds pass. The skies continue to darken.*

SCONCE   (*Pointing.*) A pair of squirrels. (*Pause.*) In love.

PRISMATIC   (*Indicating* GROVE.) Pan he *is*. Or Bacchus.

SCONCE   You mean Cupid.

PRISMATIC   I mean Pan. Or Bacchus.

SCONCE   But Cupid is the god of love.

PRISMATIC   (*Indicating the squirrels.*) This does not look like love.

SCONCE   You are concentrating on the surface.

PRISMATIC   So are they.

PYX   I am this Bacchus.

GROVE   Pounce!

SCONCE   You wish us to interrupt them?

GROVE   While they are preoccupied.

SCONCE   It does not seem humane.

GROVE   I thought you were hungry.

PRISMATIC   Not this hungry.

He exits. The others follow. The lights continue to dim, the sky almost black with clouds. The men reenter.

PRISMATIC   We have lost the road.

GROVE   The road to the coast?

PRISMATIC   The road that might lead to the road to the coast.

SCONCE   Let us retrace our steps.

PRISMATIC   We have been retracing them.

SCONCE   We will come upon it soon.

PRISMATIC   Is that right?

SCONCE   It is.

They exit and reenter. The wind picks up.

SCONCE   I do not recall this fork in the path.

GROVE   Perhaps it was not here before.

SCONCE   We will each set out in a different direction, then return to confer.

GROVE   One of us might walk for days, the others be kept waiting.

SCONCE   If you do not find it after a couple of hours, you may turn around.

GROVE   I have no conception of time.

PYX   I am these paths.

PRISMATIC   Grenadine!

SCONCE   Perhaps you could play your fiddle, and we could see from which path the squirrels come running.

GROVE   They will have separated by now.

SCONCE   So you, too, maintain it was not love.

GROVE   Love or not, they will have separated by now.

They exit. The wind continues to rise, howling now. The sound of rain. The men reenter.

GROVE   I nearly walked into that tree.

SCONCE   Single file.

GROVE   That is the ruin of the lemmings.

SCONCE   We are not lemmings.

PRISMATIC   Not yet.

They exit. The rain stops, and twilight comes. The men reenter.

GROVE   Is this not the fork again?

SCONCE   Are we sure it is the same one?

PRISMATIC   What does it matter if it is the same one!

SCONCE   How else will we know if we have made progress?

PRISMATIC   Our progress does not depend on the total number of forks but on the particular prong that leads to the road.

PYX   I am this progress.

He begins to pile sticks for a fire.

GROVE   What is Pyx doing?

SCONCE   He is building a fire.

GROVE   The sticks are wet.

SCONCE   It was only a light rain, and it has stopped. We will help him. It will give our minds some time to rest.

PRISMATIC   To rest from what?

SCONCE   From our choice of paths. Perhaps then, with our minds clear, we will remember the path to the road.

GROVE   How many sticks do we require?

SCONCE   His flame must soar to the firmament.

PYX   I am this center.

PRISMATIC   Have you done this before? You have not forgotten our precedent of failure?

SCONCE   We may take from his light.

PRISMATIC   What may we take from it?

SCONCE   Its eternal flame.

PYX   I am this unfolding.

SCONCE   Where would we be without the wisdom of Pyx?

PRISMATIC   We could be doing worse?

SCONCE   He is clarity itself, always of one mind.

PRISMATIC   He says he is all things.

SCONCE   Hence, of one mind.

PRISMATIC   I am going to sleep.

PRISMATIC *lies down. The lights dim to total darkness. Pause.*

GROVE   Shall I keep gathering sticks?

PYX   I am this upheaval.

The sound of sticks scraping against one another.

GROVE   Does this really work?

SCONCE   You must have faith.

GROVE   My top stick keeps sliding off my bottom one.

SCONCE   You must be steadfast.

GROVE   It is my sticks that are sliding, not I.

PRISMATIC   Be quiet, all three of you.

SCONCE   In fairness to Pyx, he has not spoken.

PRISMATIC   He will speak soon.

PYX   I am this fairness.

GROVE   Is that smoke near Pyx I see?

PYX   I am this smoke.

GROVE   I do not believe it.

SCONCE   It is spreading through the pile.

GROVE   Is that a flame?

PYX   I am that flame.

GROVE   He has done it!

An orange glow begins to fill the stage. A crackling sound, growing louder.

PYX   I am this fire!

PRISMATIC   What is happening?

SCONCE   Trust in Pyx, I tell you.

GROVE   Is that the road I see?

PRISMATIC   The road!

PYX   I am this consummation!

PRISMATIC *runs off.* SCONCE, GROVE, *and* PYX *follow. The orange light fades.*

Scene Four

The lights rise on the MASTER OF CEREMONIES, *wearing top hat and tails, standing before a curtain at the edge of the stage.* PRISMATIC, SCONCE, GROVE, *and* PYX *enter.*

MASTER OF CEREMONIES Welcome, gentlemen! One dollar per person. Food and entertainment included.

PRISMATIC (*Taking out his money.*) Three dollars is all we have left.

SCONCE You three go.

GROVE No, I will stay.

PRISMATIC (*To the* MASTER OF CEREMONIES.) Perhaps you could make an exception for us.

MASTER OF CEREMONIES I must treat everyone the same.

The ELDER DUCK, YOUNGER DUCK, *and* TURTLE *enter. They carry their respective animal costumes.*

MASTER OF CEREMONIES Welcome, my friends!

He opens the curtain, and they walk in without paying.

PRISMATIC Why did you not treat them the same?

MASTER OF CEREMONIES They are participants.

PRISMATIC   We are participants.

MASTER OF CEREMONIES   What will you be doing?

PRISMATIC   Whatever is being done.

MASTER OF CEREMONIES   There are many things
being done.

PRISMATIC   We will do them.

MASTER OF CEREMONIES   Which?

PRISMATIC   Whichever.

MASTER OF CEREMONIES   You must tell me your
talent, or I will not be able to introduce you. That is how
a talent show works.

GROVE   Is this a talent show, then?

PRISMATIC   He plays the fiddle, we are his dancing
accompaniment.

MASTER OF CEREMONIES   You do not look like
dancers to me.

PRISMATIC   The judges will decide.

MASTER OF CEREMONIES   Why did you not tell me
when you arrived that you were participants?

PRISMATIC   Why did you not ask us when we arrived?

MASTER OF CEREMONIES   It seems suspicious, you
must admit.

PRISMATIC *You* seem suspicious. You have not even told us where the food is.

MASTER OF CEREMONIES You will see it when you walk in. You have ten minutes before we start.

PRISMATIC, SCONCE, GROVE, *and* PYX *pass through the curtain. The lights fade, then rise a few minutes later on the* MASTER OF CEREMONIES, *tapping a microphone.* PRISMATIC, SCONCE, GROVE, *and* PYX *stand off to the side, along with the* DUCKS *and the* TURTLE, *who are in their animal costumes, with the heads still in their hands.*

GROVE I am nervous.

PRISMATIC You do not have to perform. I only said that so we could eat. We can leave now.

He starts to go.

GROVE But I want to perform. All my life I have wanted to perform for an audience.

PYX I am this dancer.

MASTER OF CEREMONIES (*To the audience.*) We will begin today with an acting troupe who will be performing—

(*He puts his hand over the microphone, to the* TURTLE.) What will you be performing?

TURTLE *The Fate of the Turtle.*

MASTER OF CEREMONIES (*To the audience.*) *The Fate of the Turtle.*

The DUCKS *and the* TURTLE *put on their animal heads, assume center stage.*

ELDER DUCK   (*To the* YOUNGER DUCK.) The lake is
drying up. If we do not fly away and seek a new home,
we will die of thirst. We must tell our friend, the turtle,
of our plan and bid him farewell.

SCONCE   He is no turtle.

MASTER OF CEREMONIES   Shhh!

SCONCE   "Shhh!" all you want, he is no turtle, the
others are no ducks. I saw them put on those heads.

The DUCKS *approach the* TURTLE.

TURTLE   Ah! Here you are. I began to wonder if I was
ever going to see you again, for somehow, though the lake
has grown smaller, I seem to have grown weaker, and it is
lonely spending all day and night by oneself.

ELDER DUCK   Oh, my friend, I have something to tell
you that I fear will cause you greater pain still. If we do
not wish to die of thirst, we must leave this place at once.
My heart bleeds to say this, for there is nothing—nothing
else in the world—that would have induced us to part
from you.

TURTLE   How can you think I am able to live without
you, when for so long you have been my only friends? If
you leave me, death will speedily put an end to my grief.

YOUNGER DUCK   Our sorrow is as great as yours, but
what can we do? And remember that if we are not here to
drink the water, there will be more for you.

TURTLE   Water is as necessary to me as to you, and if
death stares in your faces, it stares in mine also. In the
name of all the years we have passed together, do not,

I beseech you, leave me to perish here alone. Wherever you may go, take me with you.

ELDER DUCK How can we do what you ask? Our bodies, like yours, are heavy and our feet small. Our only hope lies in our wings—and alas, you cannot fly.

TURTLE No, I cannot fly, but you are so clever. Surely you can think of a plan.

ELDER DUCK Take this stick firmly in your mouth, and however high above the earth you find yourself, do not move your feet or open your mouth.

TURTLE I promise not to move head or foot and never to speak a word during the whole journey.

SCONCE This plan is not sound.

MASTER OF CEREMONIES Shhh!

PRISMATIC I did not get enough to eat.

GROVE They will throw us out.

PYX I am this journey.

The DUCKS *tie an imaginary stick to their necks, and the* TURTLE *stands between them and takes the stick in his mouth. The* DUCKS *begin to flap their wings, pretending to fly across the stage; a few areas of smoke indicate clouds and streaks of sunlight.*

YOUNGER DUCK (*Looking down.*) What are those people saying down there?

ELDER DUCK They are saying what a burden the turtle must be.

The TURTLE *looks anxiously from one* DUCK *to the other, struggling not to move or speak.*

ELDER DUCK   Do not worry. You are not a burden.

YOUNGER DUCK   (*Looking down.*) What are they saying now?

ELDER DUCK   They are saying how selfish he must be.

The TURTLE *looks anxiously from one* DUCK *to the other.*

ELDER DUCK   Do not worry. You are not selfish.

YOUNGER DUCK   (*Looking down.*) What are they saying now?

ELDER DUCK   They are saying how sorry we must be to have brought him.

The TURTLE *looks anxiously from one* DUCK *to the other.*

ELDER DUCK   Do not worry. We are not sorry.

TURTLE   Am I a burden?

He falls, his words tailing off. The lights fade, then rise on the DUCKS, *flying alone, looking down.*

ELDER DUCK   Come, we can let go of the stick.

The DUCKS *drop the imaginary stick.*

PYX   I am this stick.

ELDER DUCK   We feared it would end so, yet perhaps our friend was right to come with us. Even this death was better than the one which awaited him.

SCONCE   (*To the* DUCKS.) I told you your plan was not sound!

PRISMATIC   I am going back for more food.

MASTER OF CEREMONIES   Out! All of you!

PRISMATIC, SCONCE, GROVE, *and* PYX *exit. The lights fade, then rise on the four men standing outside.*

GROVE   One does not speak during a performance.

SCONCE   He was no turtle, and their plan was not sound.

PRISMATIC   You three took all the food for yourselves.

GROVE   All my life I have wanted to perform for an audience.

PYX   I am this audience.

PRISMATIC   We will sleep here tonight.

SCONCE   It is midday.

PRISMATIC   I am too hungry to proceed. No one even brought me a sandwich.

SCONCE   Would you like us to carry you on our shoulders?

PRISMATIC   I would not.

He lies down. The others stand around him. The lights fade.

Scene Five

The four men stand in front of a sign that reads, "Welcome Dotsuns."

PRISMATIC We will follow this sign. There is sure to be food.

GROVE We are not Dachshunds.

PRISMATIC It says "Dotsuns."

SCONCE We are not Dotsuns, either.

PRISMATIC For now we are. Sconce Dotsun, Grove Dotsun, Pyx Dotsun, Prismatic Dotsun.

PYX I am this Dotsun.

PRISMATIC Very good, Pyx.

The men walk offstage. The lights fade, then rise on a picnic table covered with a tablecloth and bowls of food. NESSA *and* FERGUS DOTSUN *stand near it, a few feet apart.* PRISMATIC, SCONCE, GROVE, *and* PYX *enter.*

GROVE They do not look like dachshunds.

PRISMATIC That is because they are Dotsuns.

SCONCE You are both mistaken. This is the House of Ulster. Note the pattern on the tablecloth, the pattern of the Ulsters.

GROVE   The ancient Celts?

PRISMATIC   For the next half hour these are the
Dotsuns, and we are their relatives.

PYX   I am this Dotsun.

PRISMATIC   Listen to Pyx.

He walks toward the picnic table. The others follow.

NESSA   Are you with Fergus's side of the family?

PRISMATIC   Prismatic Dotsun. These are my cousins.
Sconce Dotsun, Grove Dotsun, Pyx Dotsun.

NESSA   Let me get Fergus for you.

PRISMATIC   Do not trouble yourself.

NESSA   Fergus.

FERGUS *walks over.*

PRISMATIC   I was referring to the other Fergus.

FERGUS   There is no other Fergus.

PRISMATIC   He is easily forgotten, I admit.

FERGUS   I do not know any of you, either.

PRISMATIC   We ourselves are easily forgotten.

FERGUS   I ask you to leave

PYX   I was this Dotsun.

PRISMATIC   Do not think I will not tell the other
Fergus.

He starts to walk off. SCONCE, GROVE, *and* PYX *follow.*
PRISMATIC *stops at the edge of the stage.*

PRISMATIC   We must divert them. (*To* GROVE.) You will
now have your chance to play your fiddle for an audience.

GROVE   Did they request a performance?

PRISMATIC   You will play behind that tree. When they
hear the music—

SCONCE   They will copulate like the squirrels?

PRISMATIC   No, but they will turn to see where it is
coming from and approach it out of curiosity.

GROVE   You honor me.

PRISMATIC   Your music. The rest of us will run off with
as many bowls as we can. Stop playing and wait for us to
disappear.

GROVE   Will they not be surprised?

PRISMATIC   Once they have turned around and
resumed their conversations, quietly make your way to
the road.

GROVE   Will they not notice the missing bowls?

PRISMATIC   We will have run off by then.

GROVE   The three of you, yes, but—

PRISMATIC   If you wait for them to turn around and quietly make your way to the road—

GROVE   What if they do not turn around but instead pursue the origin of the sound?

PRISMATIC   Play your fiddle.

GROVE   I do not know the song of the Dachshunds.

PRISMATIC   Do *Dotsun* and *Dachshund* really sound the same to you?

GROVE   Not to me, but I am only one man.

PRISMATIC   Play.

GROVE *walks a few paces away and begins to play.*

PRISMATIC   (TO FERGUS *and* NESSA.) Turn, damn you.

SCONCE   Perhaps they do not hear the music.

PRISMATIC   They are closer to it than we are.

SCONCE   Perhaps our hearing is superior.

FERGUS *and* NESSA *take the picnic table off the stage.*

SCONCE   They are leaving, taking the bowls with them.

PYX   I am this desertion.

PRISMATIC   Grenadine!

GROVE   Is something the matter?

SCONCE   The Ulsters have left.

PRISMATIC   Grenadine!

GROVE   Was she not gone already?

PRISMATIC   Gray, grim, grisly, gray!

The lights fade, then rise on an empty stage. The men reenter.

GROVE   Was my playing not satisfactory?

SCONCE   They could not hear you.

GROVE   Have we decided on a gift for Grenadine?

SCONCE   You are no longer giving her mittens?

PRISMATIC   I was never giving her mittens!

GROVE   Anything but a ring is still my suggestion.

SCONCE   Even last time I thought the ring unwise.

GROVE   You should have said something before we stole it.

PRISMATIC   I was proposing to her! When you propose to a woman you offer her a ring!

SCONCE   It is too conventional. It is probably why she rejected you.

PRISMATIC   She rejected me because I am unconventional.

GROVE   What is your opinion, Pyx?

PRISMATIC   You are asking him?

GROVE   We need ideas.

PRISMATIC   Not his.

SCONCE   Did Grenadine say you were unconventional?

PRISMATIC   She implied it.

SCONCE   You are a mystery, Prismatic. So particular in your daily life, and yet in love, you rely on implication.

They exit. The lights fade.

Scene Six

Early morning. PRISMATIC, SCONCE, *and* GROVE *are waking up.*

GROVE   Where is Pyx?

PRISMATIC   Over there.

SCONCE   That could be anyone.

PRISMATIC   Then it is Pyx, for he is all things.

GROVE   I see no one else.

SCONCE   That does not mean it is Pyx.

GROVE   Should we go after him?

SCONCE   What if it is not Pyx, and the actual Pyx returns, discovers that we are not here, and looks for us where we have not gone?

PRISMATIC   It will be his fault for leaving.

PRISMATIC *exits. The others follow. The day begins to brighten.* PYX *enters.*

PYX   I am this loneliness.

The others enter.

GROVE   You are not alone.

PYX *exits.*

GROVE (*To* PRISMATIC.) He is sad because you did not want his gift idea. He is in need of our companionship.

PRISMATIC It was he who left us.

GROVE He is crying out.

PRISMATIC He is always crying out.

SCONCE He is heading for the ocean.

They exit. The lights continue to brighten, glaring, dazzling.
PYX *enters.*

PYX I am this sea.

PRISMATIC, SCONCE, *and* GROVE *enter.* PYX *starts to walk off.*

SCONCE He is going into the water.

PYX I am this absence.

He exits.

GROVE I will join him, in case he gets trapped in the coral.

SCONCE One does not get trapped in coral.

PRISMATIC Pyx might.

GROVE Will you go with us?

PRISMATIC I have been swimming with you once already.

SCONCE *and* GROVE *strip down to their briefs.*

PRISMATIC   Forgive us.

GROVE   Is it our ugliness you refer to?

PRISMATIC   You were ugly with your clothes on, but with them off—

SCONCE   Are we as ugly as that?

PRISMATIC   Uglier.

SCONCE   To the sea!

GROVE   To the sea!

GROVE *and* SCONCE *exit.* PRISMATIC *sits on the sand.*

SCONCE   (*Offstage.*) The water is up to his neck.

GROVE   We have not abandoned you, Pyx!

SCONCE   The water covers him.

PRISMATIC *stands.*

GROVE   I am going in.

SCONCE   Poseidon will guide us.

PRISMATIC *runs off, fully clothed. The stage is empty except for the pile of clothes and the fiddle. Several seconds pass.*

GROVE   I have him!

SCONCE   He was not easy to bring up.

PRISMATIC   It is me, you idiots!

Pause. The lights fade to sunset. PRISMATIC, SCONCE, *and* GROVE *reenter, sit, and face the ocean.*

SCONCE   We must have faith.

PRISMATIC   Have whatever you like. It has been over two hours.

GROVE   Is that too long?

The lights fade to darkness, then rise. It is dawn, and the men are sitting as they were, still gazing at the sea.

GROVE   Perhaps we should say a few words, to let him know we think well of him.

PRISMATIC   Even when Pyx was alive it was difficult to convey information to him.

SCONCE   (*To* GROVE.) Play your fiddle. He will shout, "I am this music," and we may locate him thereby.

PRISMATIC   Pyx is done shouting.

SCONCE   We must have faith.

GROVE *plays. After a few seconds, the sound of seagulls is heard overhead.* PRISMATIC *looks up.*

PRISMATIC   Let us go.

He exits. GROVE *and* SCONCE *put on their clothes and follow. The lights fade, then rise on the* OLD MAN SITTING ON THE SIDE OF THE ROAD. PRISMATIC, SCONCE, *and* GROVE *enter.*

SCONCE   (*Aside.*) Abel, son of Adam.

PRISMATIC   Doubtful.

GROVE   Was he not killed by Cain?

SCONCE   He was kicked.

PRISMATIC   He was killed.

SCONCE   If he was killed, how do you explain his presence here?

PRISMATIC   This is not Abel.

SCONCE   (*To the* OLD MAN.) Are you Abel?

OLD MAN   Not anymore.

PRISMATIC   Can you tell us where to find some food?

OLD MAN   Down the road an old couple is selling tomatoes.

GROVE   I am a fan of tomatoes.

SCONCE   You do not seem pleased, Prismatic.

PRISMATIC   I am allergic to tomatoes.

GROVE   (*To the* OLD MAN.) Would you like to join us?

OLD MAN   I prefer to be alone.

GROVE   Have you always preferred it?

OLD MAN   Some of my companions left me, I left the others.

GROVE   We would never leave you.

OLD MAN   One seldom plans to.

GROVE   You are happy, then?

OLD MAN   I am sitting on a curb without prospects.
You need not ask whether I am happy.

SCONCE   You are a plainspoken man. We are sorry you
cannot join us.

OLD MAN   I envy your enthusiasm.

PRISMATIC   We are not enviable.

OLD MAN   You are still together.

PRISMATIC   But not enviable.

He exits. SCONCE *and* GROVE *follow. The lights fade,
then rise on the* OLD MAN *and* OLD WOMAN SELLING
TOMATOES. PRISMATIC, SCONCE, *and* GROVE *enter.*

SCONCE   (*To* PRISMATIC.) What happens when you
eat tomatoes?

PRISMATIC   My face breaks out in a rash.

SCONCE   Have you tried creams?

PRISMATIC   I do not believe there are creams for such
a rash.

SCONCE   There are creams for everything.

PRISMATIC   And where would I find them now?

SCONCE   Perhaps the old couple has some.

PRISMATIC   I have never come across a tomato stand that sells creams.

SCONCE   In certain provinces.

PRISMATIC   Not the ones I have been to.

GROVE   Why are we not enviable?

(*They approach the tomato stand.*)

OLD WOMAN   Three for a dollar.

SCONCE *and* GROVE *each pick out three tomatoes.* PRISMATIC *hands the* OLD WOMAN *two dollars.*

OLD WOMAN   None for you?

PRISMATIC   I am allergic to tomatoes.

GROVE   Succulent.

SCONCE   Succulent, indeed.

PRISMATIC *grabs a tomato and stuffs it in his mouth.*

OLD WOMAN   One dollar.

PRISMATIC *hands the* OLD WOMAN *a dollar and devours two more tomatoes.* SCONCE *and* GROVE *eat slowly, gazing at* PRISMATIC. PRISMATIC *clenches his fists, fighting the urge to scratch. He cannot resist for long and begins to scratch his face.*

GROVE   It would be better if you did not scratch.

OLD WOMAN   His face swells.

PRISMATIC   Grenadine!

GROVE   He refers to his love. Perhaps you could help us think of a gift for her.

SCONCE   Tell him an engagement ring is too conventional.

GROVE   She declined the first one, which we stole from a pawn shop.

OLD WOMAN   My husband, too, did not have enough money for a ring, so he put his finger around my own and said he would keep it there always if I wished.

GROVE   (*To* SCONCE.) That is a much better idea.

SCONCE   We are not as smart as we seem.

PRISMATIC   Grenadine!

OLD WOMAN   What is her occupation?

GROVE   She worked at the pier with the four of us.

OLD WOMAN   There are only three of you.

GROVE   Forgive me, there used to be four. She operated the carousel. The four of us were custodians.

OLD WOMAN   Perhaps he could give her a ceramic pony.

GROVE   He has given her horses before. He would spend his wages, often our wages too, on the games at the pier, throwing rings around the green bottles, flipping frogs onto lily pads, knocking over tin cans. Afterward, he would bring her the horses he had won. She said she wanted real horses, not the lifeless ones of the pier.

OLD WOMAN   If she did not want those horses, why did he keep bringing her more?

GROVE   He could not afford real ones. He said he would steal all the horses in Camelot if she would marry him. It turned out she was not interested in the horses of Camelot but in the ones in the park overlooking the pier.

OLD WOMAN   (*To the* OLD MAN.) If she loved him it would not matter.

The OLD MAN *nods.*

GROVE   At least we do not have to go to Camelot.

PRISMATIC   Grenadine!

The lights fade, then rise on an empty stage as the three men reenter.

GROVE   Lovely people.

SCONCE   The gentleman said little.

PRISMATIC   He said nothing.

GROVE   But was still lovely.

SCONCE   And the tomatoes were succulent.

GROVE   (*To* PRISMATIC.) How is your face?

PRISMATIC   You are looking at it.

SCONCE   It is a good thing Grenadine is not here to observe it.

GROVE   It is my belief that we are better off with blemishes, as our ugliness can be attributed thereto.

PRISMATIC   Play your fiddle.

GROVE *plays. The* GIRL *and* BOY *enter.*

SCONCE   (*Aside.*) Romulus and Remus.

PRISMATIC   Romulus and Remus were boys.

SCONCE   Remus was a girl.

PRISMATIC   He was a boy.

SCONCE   (*To the* BOY *and* GIRL.) He plays well, does he not?

The BOY *and* GIRL *smile.* GROVE *stops playing.*

GROVE   Do you like the fiddle?

GIRL   We are six.

SCONCE   You are two.

PRISMATIC   She refers to their age.

SCONCE   Then they are twelve.

GROVE   Unless they are each three.

SCONCE   They are not each three.

BOY   Are you two loons?

PRISMATIC   Keen lad.

GIRL   We never met a loon.

PRISMATIC   As you grow older.

SCONCE   As they grow older what?

PRISMATIC   They will meet more and more loons.

BOY   I want to be a loon.

GIRL   I want to be a loon, too.

PRISMATIC   Be something else.

BOY   But I want to be one.

GIRL   And I want to be one, too.

GROVE   Do you really want to be like us?

The BOY *and* GIRL *nod fervently.*

GROVE   Would you like to help us find his Grenadine?

GIRL   We are going to be loons!

PRISMATIC   They cannot come with us. They have parents and so forth.

GROVE   Everyone has parents.

The MOTHER *and* FATHER *enter.*

MOTHER Get away from them!

FATHER Did I tell you you could leave us?

MOTHER Did they touch you?

SCONCE So many questions.

PRISMATIC We did not touch them.

FATHER (*To* PRISMATIC.) Did I ask you to speak?

SCONCE If you did, I did not hear you.

FATHER I asked neither him nor you to speak.

SCONCE In all fairness we did not ask you to speak
either.

BOY We are finding Grenadine!

GIRL And becoming loons!

MOTHER Kidnappers!

FATHER You think you can take our children!

SCONCE It would have been possible, but Prismatic
would not let us because he said they had parents and
sofas.

GROVE He did not say "sofas," he said "so forth."

SCONCE I do not know this so forth.

The MOTHER *and* FATHER *pull the* GIRL *and* BOY *away.*

BOY   But I want to go with them!

GIRL   I want to be a loon!

The GIRL *and* BOY *exit with their* MOTHER *and* FATHER.
PRISMATIC, SCONCE, *and* GROVE *look on. The lights fade.*

Scene Seven

The lights rise on SCONCE *kneeling before a plant.* PRISMATIC *and* GROVE *stand behind him.*

SCONCE   This plant is edible and also has several medicinal properties. I know of no better remedy for reducing a fever, especially if the fever is accompanied by dizziness, nausea, shortness of breath, and cramps.

GROVE   Quite the fever.

SCONCE   When Sir Galahad—

PRISMATIC   Sir Galahad?

SCONCE   When Sir Galahad was taken with such a fever, we fed him the leaves and stems of this plant, for both are edible, and not only did it alleviate his infirmity, it also removed his wart.

PRISMATIC   Sir Galahad had a wart?

SCONCE   On his thumb.

GROVE   I have a wart on my thumb.

SCONCE   This plant would remove it.

PRISMATIC   Do not listen to him.

GROVE   You are fond of my wart?

PRISMATIC   It is not your wart that concerns me.

SCONCE   Galahad, too, had reservations.

PRISMATIC   I want you to think for a moment, Grove. I want you to think of Sconce, and of this plant, and of Galahad most of all.

GROVE   I realize I am not his equal, but our warts are similarly placed.

SCONCE   His was on the other thumb, but that should not make a difference.

GROVE *takes a bite from the plant. The lights fade, then rise a moment later.*

GROVE   I do not feel well.

PRISMATIC   He has a temperature.

SCONCE   We all do.

GROVE   I am also a bit dizzy.

SCONCE   Give it time.

GROVE   Seasick.

PRISMATIC   He begins to sweat.

GROVE   Short of breath.

SCONCE   Have patience.

GROVE   Cramps.

PRISMATIC   You are killing Grove!

GROVE   My wart remains.

SCONCE   Perhaps you need both the fever and the wart.

GROVE   I *have* both the fever and the wart.

SCONCE   I mean before you eat the plant.

GROVE   If you think so.

PRISMATIC   Grenadine!

GROVE *takes another bite from the plant. The lights fade, then rise.*

PRISMATIC   He is practically yellow.

GROVE   I feel worse.

SCONCE   I cannot explain it.

PRISMATIC   Would you like me to help you?

SCONCE   Perhaps he should have eaten only the stems.

PRISMATIC   I will not allow you to feed him more of this plant.

SCONCE   You wish him to remain sick?

GROVE   I am this plant!

SCONCE   Do you know what this means?

PRISMATIC   He is hallucinating.

SCONCE   He sounds like Pyx.

GROVE   I am this illness!

SCONCE   Perhaps since Pyx is all things he is now Grove,
and with this plant we have recovered them both.

GROVE   Grenadine!

SCONCE   We have found her!

GROVE   Do you hear my cries and my shouts and
my lamentations and my fears?

SCONCE   He is turning into you too now.

GROVE   We are not as smart as we seem!

PRISMATIC   And into you.

SCONCE   It is difficult to decipher indeed.

PRISMATIC *puts his arm around* GROVE.

PRISMATIC   Help me support him.

SCONCE   It is beyond my reckoning.

PRISMATIC   There is much beyond your reckoning.

SCONCE   Sir Galahad could not have lived without
my help.

PRISMATIC   If only the rest of us were as fortunate.

PRISMATIC *and* SCONCE *help* GROVE *off. The lights fade.*

Scene Eight

The SISTER OF THE BRIDE, FATHER OF THE BRIDE, *and* MOTHER OF THE BRIDE *are standing around nervously.* PRISMATIC, SCONCE, *and* GROVE *enter.*

SISTER OF THE BRIDE Are you the band?

FATHER OF THE BRIDE Did we not hire more than just a fiddler?

MOTHER OF THE BRIDE They are vagrants.

GROVE We have been called ugly, too.

SISTER OF THE BRIDE I think the fiddle a beautiful instrument.

FATHER OF THE BRIDE Tell your sister the music has arrived.

The FATHER *and* MOTHER OF THE BRIDE *exit. The* SISTER OF THE BRIDE *lingers for a moment, gazing at* GROVE.

PRISMATIC (*To* SCONCE.) Do you notice this?

SCONCE She thinks the fiddle a beautiful instrument.

PRISMATIC But Grove?

SCONCE He is a handsome man.

PRISMATIC He is not.

The SISTER OF THE BRIDE *exits.*

GROVE   I do not know what to play.

SCONCE   Your fiddle.

The three men exit. The lights fade.

Scene Nine

The lights rise on GROVE *playing his fiddle.* SCONCE *dances frantically with the* MOTHER OF THE BRIDE, *swinging her around.* PRISMATIC *and the* FATHER OF THE BRIDE *stand off to the side. The* SISTER OF THE BRIDE *gazes at* GROVE.

PRISMATIC   He plays well, does he not?

FATHER OF THE BRIDE   Indeed, but I still maintain I hired more than just a fiddler.

PRISMATIC   Is there something wrong with your other daughter?

FATHER OF THE BRIDE   She prefers unattractive men. I suppose because of me.

PRISMATIC   You are one thing, Grove another.

MOTHER OF THE BRIDE   Help!

FATHER OF THE BRIDE   Should I worry about your other companion?

PRISMATIC   He thinks he helped Galahad search for the Grail.

FATHER OF THE BRIDE   It is good to exercise the imagination.

PRISMATIC   Sconce does more than exercise it.

FATHER OF THE BRIDE   Too often we distrust our imaginations.

PRISMATIC   Sconce trusts nothing else.

FATHER OF THE BRIDE   More of us should think we traveled with Galahad.

GROVE *stops playing.* SCONCE *stops swinging the* MOTHER OF THE BRIDE *around, and she totters about the stage until the* FATHER OF THE BRIDE *helps her offstage. The* SISTER OF THE BRIDE *continues to gaze at* GROVE.

SISTER OF THE BRIDE   (*To* GROVE.) Where are you going now?

GROVE *does not respond.*

PRISMATIC   Answer her, Grove.

SISTER OF THE BRIDE   (*To* GROVE.) I was hoping you would be staying here for awhile.

GROVE *remains speechless.*

PRISMATIC   Go to it, Grove.

GROVE   We are searching for his Grenadine.

PRISMATIC   Stop it, Grove!

GROVE   What is it?

PRISMATIC   Consider the odds that a young woman with a fondness for fiddles, of fine appearance, of adequate means, of good health—

SCONCE   Do we know whether she is in good health?

PRISMATIC Likes you, Grove, in spite of your unsavory appearance, your lack of means, your lack of good health. Consider the odds!

GROVE Are they that small?

PRISMATIC Smaller!

GROVE You are my friends.

PRISMATIC Forget us! Just look at us for a moment!

SCONCE How can he forget us if he is to look at us?

GROVE I have already looked at you.

SCONCE He is looking at us even now.

PRISMATIC How could you possibly wish to remain with us? We are unsightly, unseemly, untenable.

SCONCE You present a foul portrait.

PRISMATIC We are a foul portrait!

GROVE I do not know.

The MOTHER *and* FATHER OF THE BRIDE *enter.*

SISTER OF THE BRIDE I have to go soon.

GROVE I have no conception of time.

PRISMATIC Damn it, Grove!

SISTER OF THE BRIDE You can stay in my sister's room.

The MOTHER OF THE BRIDE *whimpers. The* FATHER OF
THE BRIDE *helps her offstage.*

GROVE   (*To* PRISMATIC.) You do not want me to come
with you?

PRISMATIC   You have come with us long enough.

GROVE   You are my friends.

PRISMATIC   I command you, Grove.

GROVE *walks off with the* SISTER OF THE BRIDE, *then stops
at the edge of the stage and turns around.*

GROVE   I will remember you.

PRISMATIC   Forget us, as we will forget you.

GROVE *exits with the* SISTER OF THE BRIDE.

SCONCE   You were unkind to Grove.

PRISMATIC   No one has ever been kinder to him.

(*He bends over in pain.*)

SCONCE   Did I not tell you to eat less?

PRISMATIC   It had been days since I had eaten.

SCONCE   You will listen to me next time.

PRISMATIC   I will kill you when I have the strength.

SCONCE   Cuchulainn was a fractious companion, but,
I maintain, no more fractious than you.

PRISMATIC   Cuchulainn? The Irish Achilles?

SCONCE   The noblest of the Ulsters, and as irritable as
a goat.

PRISMATIC   You knew him?

SCONCE   I remember once he slapped me for no reason.

PRISMATIC   I can think of several reasons he may have
slapped you.

SCONCE   "Why did you just slap me?" I asked him. But
he did not know why he had just slapped me.

PRISMATIC   Had you been speaking, because I find that
when you speak—

SCONCE   I moved to the other side of our group, but
he followed me and slapped me again. "You have slapped
me again," I said. "I have," said Cuchulainn. I returned to
the other side of our group. He followed me and slapped
me a third time. "Is there no stopping this?" I asked. "It
is impossible to say," said Cuchulainn. I paused and waited
for him to advance with the rest of our group, but he
remained beside me. At last I set out, and he slapped me
once more.

PRISMATIC   There he cannot be blamed.

PRISMATIC *exits.* SCONCE *follows. The lights fade.*

Scene Ten

The OLD WOMAN PAINTING A LANDSCAPE *is seated by her easel.* PRISMATIC *and* SCONCE *enter.*

SCONCE (*Aside.*) Sibyl.

PRISMATIC I no longer respond to this.

SCONCE You deny my report?

PRISMATIC Sibyl, the seer?

SCONCE She.

PRISMATIC Whom Apollo gave eternal life?

SCONCE Would she be here if he had not?

PRISMATIC Who forgot to ask for eternal youth?

SCONCE Do you not detect her aged appearance?

PRISMATIC This is that Sibyl?

SCONCE Who else?

PRISMATIC (*To the* OLD WOMAN.) Sibyl.

The OLD WOMAN *does not reply.*

PRISMATIC (*To* SCONCE.) Sibyl forgot to ask for eternal hearing, too.

SCONCE   Sibyl does not respond, because you have no faith.

PRISMATIC   (*To the* OLD WOMAN.) Sibyl, if I had faith, would you respond to me?

SCONCE   You cannot trick Sibyl.

PRISMATIC   You cannot do anything to Sibyl.

SCONCE   I believe I know what the trouble is.

PRISMATIC   This is not Sibyl.

SCONCE   As Sibyl began to age, we began to lose confidence in her powers of prediction.

PRISMATIC   We?

SCONCE   As she grew older, we no longer consulted her, so that now, though her augury be as potent as before, she refuses to answer.

PRISMATIC   You think that this woman before us, painting this landscape, is Sybil, the seer, who pretends not to hear us because we doubt her prophesies, on account of her shrunken appearance, apropos of her misunderstanding with Apollo two thousand five hundred years ago over the meaning of eternity?

SCONCE   Is there another explanation?

OLD WOMAN   (*Suddenly turning on them.*) How long do you two nincompoops plan to stand above me and waste my day with your words? I come here for silence and serenity, and instead I am subjected to two idiots insulting my appearance and disturbing me in the modest pursuit of my work.

PRISMATIC   I apologize. You will appreciate the
difficulty I have dealing with this imbecile.

OLD WOMAN   I daresay it is no easier to deal with you.

SCONCE   Prismatic has his faults, especially his
irritability, equal to that of Cuchulainn, but he is a good
man, Sybil, and together you and I, who have never denied
your power of prophesy, can convince him that though
you shrivel to a ball of string, it is better to seek you before
any Cassandra, fair and lithe though she be.

PRISMATIC   (*To the* OLD WOMAN.) You do not believe
he is more difficult to deal with?

OLD WOMAN   He has finished speaking, you have not.

SCONCE   We will go now. I have said what needed to be
said.

SCONCE *exits, and* PRISMATIC *grumblingly follows. The lights
fade, then rise on the empty stage as* PRISMATIC *and* SCONCE
reenter.

SCONCE   She reminds me in her perseverance of
Cuchulainn. In his final battle he was cudgeled in the
abdomen.

PRISMATIC   Every word of yours is like a cudgel to the
abdomen.

SCONCE   In order to keep fighting he strapped himself
to a rock.

PRISMATIC   In the middle of battle?

SCONCE   How else?

PRISMATIC   His combatants simply waited for him?

SCONCE   I do not understand your question.

PRISMATIC   Why did someone not cudgel his head
while he was strapping himself to the rock?

SCONCE   You underestimate Cuchulainn's ability.

PRISMATIC   Someone managed to cudgel his abdomen.

SCONCE   Cuchulainn did combat with fifty men at once.

PRISMATIC   All the more reason someone ought to
have cudgeled his head as he strapped himself to the rock.

SCONCE   May I continue?

PRISMATIC   You acknowledge my point.

SCONCE   I acknowledge your lack of faith.

They exit. The lights fade to early evening. PRISMATIC *and*
SCONCE *reenter.*

PRISMATIC   I thought you were going to continue.

SCONCE   I will not allow you to insult Cuchulainn.

PRISMATIC   I was not insulting him. I was questioning
his ability to fight off fifty men while strapping himself to
a rock.

SCONCE   Cuchulainn was trained by Scathach.

PRISMATIC   Regardless of who trained him, to strap
oneself to a rock requires both hands, and I do not see

how a man without hands can fight off fifty men with cudgels.

SCONCE   Scathach taught him how to jump.

PRISMATIC   There too I am in doubt, for I do not see how one can jump effectively after having been cudgeled in the abdomen.

SCONCE   That is why I speak of his perseverance. He fought until all his blood had run from him.

PRISMATIC   I thought you said he was cudgeled.

SCONCE   It was a spiked cudgel.

PRISMATIC   A spiked cudgel! And still no one could strike him as he strapped himself to the rock.

SCONCE   I speak of the death of a great warrior and friend, and you can only mock.

PRISMATIC   You consider him your friend though he slapped you in the face for no reason?

SCONCE   I consider you my friend, though your mockery hurts worse than any hand.

They exit. The lights fade.

Scene Eleven

The BEEKEEPER *is standing before a hive in his protective gear. The sound of swarming bees is heard.* PRISMATIC *and* SCONCE *enter.*

PRISMATIC Good afternoon.

BEEKEEPER You are agitating the bees.

PRISMATIC Is it not their normal state to be agitated?

BEEKEEPER Move along.

PRISMATIC May we take a jar of honey?

BEEKEEPER You may not.

He exits.

PRISMATIC (*To* SCONCE, *pointing offstage.*) The honey must be in that shanty.

SCONCE We will ask the beekeeper to reconsider when he returns.

PRISMATIC We will not wait for him to say no.

SCONCE We cannot know what he will say until we ask.

PRISMATIC We will argue about this later.

He walks off. SCONCE *follows. Their ensuing dialogue takes place offstage.*

PRISMATIC Help me carry them.

SCONCE We have gained nothing from stealing.

PRISMATIC We have gained nothing from starving.

BEEKEEPER Did I not tell you to move along?

PRISMATIC So many jars remain to you, let us take these two.

BEEKEEPER You have five seconds before I set these bees upon you.

SCONCE If Grove were here he would tell you he had no conception of time.

PRISMATIC I have not seen my love in years. If I do not eat soon—

BEEKEEPER What is your love to me?

PRISMATIC What are two jars of honey to you?

BEEKEEPER More than your love.

SCONCE Has it not been five seconds?

BEEKEEPER It has.

PRISMATIC Two jars, damn you!

The sound of swarming bees is heard. It becomes much louder as PRISMATIC *and* SCONCE *reenter and race across the stage,* PRISMATIC *carrying two jars of honey.*

SCONCE   No crime of ours goes unpunished!

PRISMATIC   You are the punishment!

They exit. The sound of bees fades. The lights fade, then rise as PRISMATIC *and* SCONCE *reenter, run onto the stage, and collapse.* PRISMATIC *tries in vain to open one of the jars. He looks at his hands.*

PRISMATIC   How long will it take for this swelling to go down?

SCONCE   Several hours, I maintain.

PRISMATIC   I shall wait until morning, then.

The lights fade, then rise to dawn. PRISMATIC *is sleeping.* SCONCE *sits a few feet away.* PRISMATIC *wakes up and looks around.*

PRISMATIC   Where is the honey?

SCONCE   I love you, Prismatic.

PRISMATIC   Where is the honey, damn you!

SCONCE   In the sea.

PRISMATIC   In the what!

SCONCE   I would have returned it to the beekeeper, but you might have gone looking for me, and we might not have found each other.

PRISMATIC   You think I would have gone looking for you!

SCONCE   We can ask the beekeeper to reconsider now.

PRISMATIC   Why are you doing this to me!

SCONCE   We are not thieves.

PRISMATIC   Why are you starving me!

SCONCE   There will be more food.

PRISMATIC   I am leaving you!

He starts to go. SCONCE *starts to follow.*

PRISMATIC   Do not follow me.

He exits. SCONCE *remains where he is. The lights fade.*

Scene Twelve

PRISMATIC *enters.*

PRISMATIC   Idiot! How improved is my situation.
No faith, he tells me. No faith in that imbecile. I would
never have found you, Grenadine. Now we will be
reunited. I can almost see you.

He exits. The lights fade to sunset. He reenters.

I have to get off this road. I have to go where there are
more people. Do not worry, Grenadine, I will find a side
road, and we will be reunited. I will bring you a sunflower.
I do not know where I will find one of those, either. But
I will find one. A sunflower and a side road. For my
gossamer gay gosling. For my sun. For my Grenadine.

He exits. The lights fade to twilight. He reenters.

Where is everyone? I know there are more people on the
earth than this. Deserts have more people. Hello there!
Anyone? Perhaps this is a desert. But I cannot go back.
That idiot might want to rejoin me. Not that I would let
him. I am free of him, of him and of his fellow idiots. If
only I could find a side road, and a sunflower.

He exits. The lights fade to moonlight. He reenters.

Where am I? There still must be cities on this earth. Any
sign of life would be positive. Have you thought of me
often, Grenadine?

"Grenadine" echoes back to him. PRISMATIC *stops.*

Play your fiddle, Grove. (*Pause.*) I said, Play your fiddle.
(*He turns to where he expects* GROVE *to be.*) It is getting late.
(*He lies down.*) How much better I shall sleep without
them.

The lights fade.

Scene Thirteen

Dawn. PRISMATIC *is sleeping. The* TWO-LEGGED
DACHSHUND *rests beside him, a buggy attached behind
him to carry his hind legs.* PRISMATIC *rises.*

PRISMATIC Welcome, Dotsun. How was the picnic?
I suppose you cannot speak.

The DACHSHUND *takes a few steps closer to* PRISMATIC, *and
the buggy wheels squeak as he struggles forward.*

You must be hungry.

The DACHSHUND *barks feebly.*

Control your excitement. I have had little success in
obtaining food, or in partaking of the right amount.
Sconce and the others, admittedly, were often impediments
to my attempts, but now it seems our prospects are fewer.
Perhaps there is a rabbit bounding about, but I do not
see you catching him in that buggy of yours. It appears
I shall have to maintain this conversation for both of us.

PRISMATIC *rises and starts to walk off. The* DACHSHUND
follows, but stops soon afterward.

I am thoughtless. Forgive me.

He attempts to pick up the DACHSHUND, *which immediately
begins to bark.*

A proud fellow. But you must try to keep up.

He walks offstage. The DACHSHUND *follows. Day begins to brighten.* PRISMATIC *and the* DACHSHUND *reenter.*

PRISMATIC   In case you are interested, we are returning to my Grenadine. At your rate, it will take us some time. But perhaps some time will make her miss me more. She is as round as the sun, and I love her. Occasionally you will hear me shout her name. Do not be startled. She is my gossamer gay gosling, and her gems are aglow. I was too hasty in my initial pursuit of her. Women do not like haste, they like slow-moving creatures like yourself. I must use you as a guide, if you do not mind.

The DACHSHUND *veers off, exiting.*

Where are you going? I have not offended you, I hope?

PRISMATIC *exits. The lights fade, then rise on a shanty. The* DACHSHUND *enters, followed by* PRISMATIC.

Good work!

PRISMATIC *walks up to the shanty and knocks. The* COOK *opens the door wearing a bloodstained apron.*

PRISMATIC   We would like something to eat.

The COOK *looks down at the* DACHSHUND.

COOK   No dogs.

PRISMATIC   We will wait out here. We do not mind.

COOK   We do not serve dogs.

PRISMATIC   You may serve me, and I will serve the dog.

COOK   We would still be serving him.

PRISMATIC   What if I promise not to do so?

COOK   You would be lying.

He closes the door.

PRISMATIC   Do not worry. We will persuade him.

He knocks. No answer.

He is assessing our fortitude.

He knocks again.

Fortitude is essential.

The COOK *opens the door.*

PRISMATIC   (*Indicating the* DACHSHUND.) Do you not perceive his injury?

COOK   We serve no dogs!

PRISMATIC   We will pay you.

COOK   How much?

PRISMATIC   No money per se, but the dog will do tricks.

COOK   With two legs?

PRISMATIC   All the more impressive the tricks.

COOK   What sort of tricks?

PRISMATIC   He will dance.

COOK   Let me see.

PRISMATIC   He must have a full stomach.

The COOK *closes the door.*

PRISMATIC   (*To the* DACHSHUND.) He is deliberating.

PRISMATIC *knocks. The* COOK *flings the door open.*

PRISMATIC   Scraps! Feed us scraps!

COOK   You have three seconds.

PRISMATIC   Three seconds is sufficient.

COOK   Get out!

PRISMATIC   We are out!

COOK   Get the hell out of here!

PRISMATIC   I already told you—

The COOK *swipes at* PRISMATIC *with the back of his hand.*
PRISMATIC *ducks. The* DACHSHUND *barks. The* COOK *slams the door.*

PRISMATIC   We will go around. There will be garbage. The difference between garbage and food is merely the presentation. If anything, garbage is superior, as it has had time to marinate.

PRISMATIC *and the* DACHSHUND *walk to the side of the shanty. The sound of buzzing flies is heard.*

Do not let the flies trouble you. They are simply pointing out to us that the beef is of good quality and suitable to our needs.

The DACHSHUND *rummages in the garbage.* PRISMATIC *bends over and picks up a plate of food.*

Maggots, too, remind us that the food is of good quality. We must remember that we are all sprung from the same earth, nurtured by the same air, the same sun, all of us mortal and regenerative, sharing a common evolutionary stage—algae, bacteria, sponges—only a few thousand years removed, according to Grove.

The DACHSHUND *remains in the garbage.*

Let us perceive it from the perspective of a child.

He picks up a piece of gristle from his plate.

Let us—

The back door opens. The COOK *stands with a garbage bag in his hand.*

PRISMATIC   You said nothing about the garbage.

COOK   You are the garbage, and I said go to hell.

The COOK *brings the garbage inside, including* PRISMATIC'*s plate, and closes the door.*

PRISMATIC   (*To the* DACHSHUND.) Come, we do not want his garbage, anyway.

He starts to walk off. The DACHSHUND *follows.*

We are too good for garbage.

They exit. The lights fade, then rise as PRISMATIC *and the*
DACHSHUND *reenter.*

PRISMATIC   That man was cruel, was he not? A
descendant of bacteria. You would have liked Grove. He
believed your kind could host picnics. Sconce, of course,
thought the hosts were Ulsters. Pyx thought the hosts
were Pyx. Pyx who is now drowned.

The DACHSHUND *stops.*

It is too early to stop. We must find a gift for Grenadine.

The DACHSHUND *slumps to the ground.*

Tomorrow you must try harder.

He sits down beside the DACHSHUND.

What do you think of mittens?

The lights fade.

Scene Fourteen

The FISHERMAN, *smoking a pipe, is tugging his boat ashore.*
PRISMATIC *and the* DACHSHUND *enter.*

PRISMATIC   A good day at sea?

FISHERMAN   A bluefin tuna. *Thunnus Thynnus.*

PRISMATIC   *Thunnus Thynnus!* It must be eight feet.

FISHERMAN   Nine.

PRISMATIC   Do you need help eating it?

FISHERMAN   I am taking it to town to sell.

PRISMATIC   There is a town?

FISHERMAN   A few miles down.

PRISMATIC   Let us help you transport it, for a small
percentage of the sale, so we can buy some food and a pair
of mittens.

FISHERMAN   (*Indicating the* DACHSHUND.) What
happened to his legs?

PRISMATIC   He found me this way. I have not seen my
love in years.

FISHERMAN   Perhaps you are not meant for each other.

PRISMATIC   Will you let us help you?

FISHERMAN   I have a buggy of my own.

PRISMATIC   That fish must be two hundred pounds.
We could take turns.

FISHERMAN   That is not necessary.

PRISMATIC   May we at least accompany you, in case
you change your mind?

FISHERMAN   I never change it.

PRISMATIC   May we accompany you, all the same?

FISHERMAN   You may not.

PRISMATIC   Have you no pity for the dachshund?

FISHERMAN   I am not fond of dogs.

PRISMATIC   The whole purpose of pity is to have it
where one is not fond.

FISHERMAN   I weary of this conversation.

PRISMATIC   We will see you in town.

PRISMATIC *exits. The* DACHSHUND *follows. The lights
fade, then rise on the empty stage as* PRISMATIC *and the*
DACHSHUND *reenter.*

PRISMATIC   Not fond of dogs. Just a few miles, you
will see. No slacking now.

They exit. The lights dim to presunset. PRISMATIC *and the*
DACHSHUND *reenter.*)

PRISMATIC   Where in hell is this town? Perhaps the fisherman has underestimated the distance, or has a strange conception of "a few."

The DACHSHUND *slumps to the ground.*

We cannot rest. We are almost there.

The GENTLEMAN *enters in a white suit, smiling and twirling a white cane.*

PRISMATIC   This gentleman will be able to tell us. Greetings. I like your suit. How far is it to the town?

GENTLEMAN   Town? There is no town in this direction.

PRISMATIC   No need for humor, my good man. You see the condition of my dog, my own, too, for that matter.

GENTLEMAN   There is only the ocean behind me.

PRISMATIC   Then where are you coming from?

GENTLEMAN   That is not a useful question.

PRISMATIC   Answer me, anyway.

GENTLEMAN   I please not to.

PRISMATIC   Stop smiling and answer my damn question.

GENTLEMAN   You are aggravated.

PRISMATIC   I would be less aggravated if you answered my question.

GENTLEMAN   I will not.

PRISMATIC   Would you like to know what I think of that suit?

GENTLEMAN   It is not necessary.

PRISMATIC   It is more than not necessary.

GENTLEMAN   I wish you all the best.

The GENTLEMAN *starts to walk off.*

PRISMATIC   To hell with you.

The GENTLEMAN *exits.*

PRISMATIC   Come, I am sure he is lying.

The DACHSHUND *gets up.* PRISMATIC *starts to walk off. The* DACHSHUND *slumps to the ground.*

I know you are tired. You think I am not tired? Do you know what Sconce would tell you? You are not a dachshund in a buggy, you are Pegasus, a winged horse. Pyx would have you say, "I am these wings, I am this Pegasus." I suspect we shall arrive before sundown, within the hour, I would say. Yes, I am convinced of it. I know they say not to be convinced of anything because then it will not come true, but to hell with them and their sayings. I fly in their faces, if you know what I mean.

He starts to go; the DACHSHUND *rises and follows.*

Yes, the sun will be setting as we turn the corner, and there it will be, like Gibraltar or Jericho or one of the others. I fly in their faces!

They exit. The lights fade, then rise on a deep orange sunset. PRISMATIC *and the* DACHSHUND *reenter.*

PRISMATIC   You see, the sun is setting. Half my prediction has come true. In a few steps we will see the town. Like Atlantis it will rise—

PRISMATIC *stops suddenly, drops to his knees. The* DACHSHUND *slumps beside him.*

Remind me to tell the fisherman there is no town in this direction. He must have run into some difficulties not to have overtaken us. Perhaps he will stumble upon us tonight, and in the morning we will share his fish. He cannot refuse us now.

The lights dim to darkness.

Scene Fifteen

Dawn. PRISMATIC *is sitting with the* DACHSHUND *resting his chin on* PRISMATIC*'s foot.*

PRISMATIC   "Come with me, Grenadine," I said. "We will live up in the Andes and raise vicuñas with our children. The huts. The huts at night, Grenadine. The sapajou monkeys and the chinchillas, the vampire bats with their crushed snouts and their fangs. We will fight them off, Grenadine." It was a beautiful speech. I do not understand how she could have given the engagement ring and the stuffed unicorn back to me.

PRISMATIC *rises.*

Come, the fisherman did not make it.

He starts off. The DACHSHUND *follows.*

We will walk along the beach. Perhaps there will be a side trail.

PRISMATIC *exits. The* DACHSHUND *follows. The lights fade, then rise on the* YOUNG MOTHER, *standing in front of a tent.* PRISMATIC *and the* DACHSHUND *enter.*

PRISMATIC   Is there a town in this direction?

The YOUNG MOTHER *puts a finger to her lips.*

PRISMATIC   (*Whispering.*) A town?

YOUNG MOTHER   About twelve miles.

PRISMATIC   (*To the* DACHSHUND.) I told you there was a town.

YOUNG MOTHER   Tell him more softly.

PRISMATIC   Do you have any food?

YOUNG MOTHER   Only for my son and me.

PRISMATIC   How old is he?

YOUNG MOTHER   Seven.

PRISMATIC   Anything at all?

YOUNG MOTHER   I only bring what is necessary.

PRISMATIC   We have not eaten in days. Well, the dachshund ate two days ago, but I—

YOUNG MOTHER   I must think of my child.

PRISMATIC   I thank you all the same, for the directions to town.

PRISMATIC *starts to go, but the* DACHSHUND *does not follow.*

PRISMATIC   (*To the* DACHSHUND.) Come, she has no food for us.

YOUNG MOTHER   Perhaps I could find him something.

PRISMATIC   (*To the* DACHSHUND.) It is only twelve miles.

YOUNG MOTHER   Just follow the path. When you
reach the main road, you have three miles to go.

PRISMATIC   (*To the* DACHSHUND.) I cannot blame you,
of course.

YOUNG MOTHER   I will take care of him.

PRISMATIC   If you see a fisherman with a large tuna,
tell him the town is this way.

PRISMATIC *exits. The lights fade, then rise on the empty stage
as he reenters.*

PRISMATIC   A kind woman. It would not have been
right to take food from the boy. And how much faster
I am moving without the dachshund. Only a few miles to
go. I should see the road soon, and then the town.

PRISMATIC *exits. The lights fade to twilight. He reenters.
The sound of seagulls and waves.* PRISMATIC *stops.*

Maybe the town is under water. Wherever you wish,
Grenadine. Antarctica or El Dorado.

PYX *enters.*

PRISMATIC   Pyx. I am reduced to hallucinations.

PYX   I am this return.

SCONCE *enters, carrying two jars of honey covered with
barnacles.*

SCONCE   I told you, with faith, he would drift ashore.

PRISMATIC   He is at the bottom of the sea.

SCONCE We did not swim out far enough.

PRISMATIC We searched for hours.

SCONCE Not out far enough. He must have joined
Nereus, wise man of the sea.

PRISMATIC I was wrong to abandon you, Sconce.

SCONCE I have been following at a safe distance. You
missed the turnoff to the main road.

PRISMATIC You might have said something.

SCONCE I thought you might still be angry with me.

PRISMATIC I am angry with you now for not saying
something.

GROVE *enters.*

GROVE Pyx?

PYX I am this companion.

GROVE What is happening?

PRISMATIC I am sorry she ended it, Grove.

GROVE It was I who left her.

PRISMATIC Then I beseech you to go back.

GROVE You are not happy to see me?

PRISMATIC We have seen you. Now go before the sight
of you becomes permanent.

GROVE   She did not need me as you need me.

PRISMATIC   As to needing you—

PYX   I am this happiness.

GROVE   Have we thought of a gift for Grenadine?

SCONCE   I have thought of several.

PRISMATIC   Play your fiddle, Grove.

SCONCE   You will not be able to hear my ideas.

PRISMATIC   Play loudly.

GROVE *plays.*

PYX   I am this music.

They exit. The lights fade. Curtain.